CHICAGO
O'HARE

PREVIOUS PAGE: Gear down, slats and flaps extended, this airliner is moments from touchdown. As with long-distance travelers on trains or buses in an earlier era, the passengers aboard this aircraft will soon disembark and begin making sales calls, participating in family reunions, touring on vacation, or any number of other activities.

RIGHT: A rare time of day when the jetways at O'Hare are vacant. This moment, in the late morning, is fleeting for an influx of airliners will soon invade the vacuum created by the flurry of departures. Meanwhile, an American Airlines F-100 cuts a swath through the sky, leaving dynamic Chicago and its incredible airport.

CHICAGO O'HARE

The World's Busiest Airport

PHILIP HANDLEMAN

MBI Publishing Company

Dedication

To the memory of Sonia Kriegmont Handleman who worked at an airport, which in its day was a major hub, and who had the spirit.

PHOTO ON FRONT COVER: Terminal 5 was built expressly for international operations. It has 156 ticket counter positions, six security checkpoints, twenty-one gates and sixty-eight immigration booths capable of processing 4,000 passengers per hour. It is a free-standing building that serves more than six million passengers annually.
(*Photo courtesy Chicago Department of Aviation*)

PHOTO ON BACK COVER: Like a giant video game, O'Hare lights up at night, radiating a fascinating quiltwork of illumination.
(*Photo courtesy Chicago Department of Aviation*)

This edition first published in 1998 by MBI Publishing Company, 729 Prospect Avenue, PO Box 1, Osceola, WI 54020-0001 USA.

© 1998 Philip Handleman

Previously published by Airlife Publishing Ltd, Shrewsbury, England.

MBI Publishing Company books are also available at discounts in bulk quantity for industrial or sales-promotional use. For details write to Special Sales Manager at Motorbooks International Wholesalers & Distributors, 729 Prospect Avenue, PO Box 1, Osceola, WI 54020-0001 USA.

Library of Congress Cataloging-in-Publication Data available

ISBN 0-7603-0685-0

Printed in Hong Kong

Acknowledgements

I am deeply indebted to those who helped me prepare this book for publication. Spending time at airports and watching airplanes is always fun, but my time at Chicago O'Hare International Airport was made especially enjoyable (and productive) by the irrepressible M.T.D.s (Motor Truck Drivers) of O'Hare's Airfield Operations unit. These hale and hardy souls unpretentiously showed me a side of the world's busiest airport almost no one gets to see. In the process, they adroitly wielded their oversize bright-yellow pickup trucks, with me aboard, so as to ensure the right camera angle for virtually every shot.

Ever mindful of the heavy flow of traffic, both ground vehicles and aircraft, they safely negotiated the obstacle course as if it were second nature. With windows rolled down and broiling summer heat gushing in, we dashed about the humming airport, sometimes chasing departing airliners and other times dodging taxying aircraft. I must have been introduced to nearly every rut, gofer hole, ditch and bump in the grassy expanses adjoining the runways and taxiways. At last, it seemed I had discovered that place called 'pilot heaven.' It was one of those rare times in life when you do not want the experience to end. Oh my, such memories to savor!

If the images of flight operations at O'Hare that follow depict some of the everyday magic of commercial air transport, then the credit ought to go to Chicago's always effervescent M.T.D.s Cliff Carlson, Joan Carter, Charlotte McGue, Kevin O'Donohue and John Recchia.

My thanks also go to Richard M. Daley, the Mayor of the City of Chicago and the personnel at the Chicago Department of Aviation, especially Cyle R. Cantrell, airport operations supervisor; Dennis Culloton, public relations; William Lonergan, deputy commissioner; Mary Rose Loney, commissioner; Stephen Nolan, public relations representative; Peter J. Schulz, photographer; and Jim Vanderhyden, public relations representative. In addition, I am grateful to Georgia Wolf, the marketing communications representative at Jeppesen Sanderson Inc.

A special note of thanks goes to my wife, Mary, whose patience with a grown man who never outgrew his childhood fascination for airplanes is remarkable. Wherever I go she is with me, my navigator in life as in flight.

Philip Handleman

Introduction

In the relentless hum of haste and commotion at today's major commercial air terminals, the greatness and wonder of airports is seldom appreciated. For baggage-laden passengers elbowing their way as they scurry down the concourses, always in a rush to get here or there, the airport is a temporary waypoint, a kind of necessary evil that must be endured to achieve the objective of getting to a chosen destination.

This scenario, playing out daily at the big city airport hubs around the world, was not always the case. In an earlier era, the air travel component of a trip was much desired and relished. If not elegant, airline flying in the old days of piston-powered aircraft was adventurous, and at times even romantic.

The very success of commercial air transport – including its unrivaled safety record, generally efficient operations and affordable prices – accounts for the disdain in which it is currently held by the public. Whereas airline flying used to be daring, it is now routine; what was for the privileged few has become commonplace for the throngs. The element of surprise, of the unknown, has all but vanished in modern airline flight operations. People dread the check-in counters and the luggage retrieval systems. Cramped boarding areas and passenger processing that resembles the machinery of a sardines cannery hardly serve as ennobling aspects.

Yet in every airport, even a saturated concrete/glass/steel monolith, there is at least a thread of that intangible prerequisite – the love of flight. Without this simple ingredient, all the rest – the terminal buildings, the hangars, the miles of runways – would lose their meaning and disappear. Each arriving and departing aircraft is there, in the most elemental way, because somewhere, somehow, certain people, not just the flight crews, developed an adoration, if not a reverence, for the world of flying and the machines that miraculously traverse the sky.

At quiet little airstrips tucked away in the far reaches of the countryside the essence of flight is at its richest, for here is where flying begins and where the airline captains and ground crew chiefs are born. Starting with a gleam in the eye at the boundary fence, the allure of flight is stimulated by the purr of a fabric-covered antique piercing the afternoon drowsiness, the unmistakable aroma of butyrate dope sharing the calm air with redolent avgas, and the radial engine of a sparkling fire-engine-red biplane bellowing smoke as it coughs to life.

A business tycoon who owned an island once sponsored an air show for the townsfolk. They came in droves to the quaint airport and watched the display from the area adjacent to the secondary runway which served as the show line. When the open-cockpit biplanes of World War Two vintage filed past in majestic procession, low and slow, the crowd spontaneously started waving to the leather-helmeted and begoggled pilots. Through the corners of their eyes the pilots could see the adulation from below, and they reciprocated by forcing their arms into the slipstream in a back and forth motion. The gesture of appreciation warmed the hearts of the spectators so much that they began to applaud.

After losing his father to an insidious disease, an adolescent was taken to a grass airstrip for his first airplane ride. Morose beyond description, the boy showed no emotion. Up he went. At altitude the pilot leveled off and began to point out local landmarks. No response; just a blank stare through the wind-screen. The pilot then demonstrated certain maneuvers, explaining the flight control inputs as he performed them. Still no response. More maneuvers with a little steeper bank, but even this elicited no response. Fearing that it was no use as this teenager could not be shaken out of his depression, the pilot descended for landing. Following the last bounce on a less than textbook touchdown, the pilot sensed something. He turned to his young passenger to find a broad grin stretched across his face.

In barnstorming fashion, a Stearman pilot headed west, following train tracks and roads, on his way to an Iowa fly-in. Low on fuel, he picked out the nearest grass strip on his flapping chart. He swooped down low over the green rectangle, a kind of oasis in a landscape dominated by cornfields extending as far as the eye could see. The airfield looked usable so he landed. He brought the venerable biplane to idle at the north end of the strip, but no one was there. He pivoted the aircraft around and taxied to the opposite end of the airfield. With the propeller still loping over, the members of an Amish family from a Victorian frame house next to the airfield darted out to greet the stranger. No, there was no fuel on site, but just a short way down the interstate, near Valparaiso, was an airport with fuel, the farmers gladly volunteered as they pointed westward. With a thumbs-up, the pilot was off to Valparaiso.

The airport is a place of aspiration, of dreaming and striving for what may come. At places like Tuskegee and Sweetwater, airports permitted dreams of valor to come true and long overdue opportunities to be taken. The airports at Duxford and Entebbe proved there is no limit to mankind's quest for freedom. In the skies over the hallowed ground of Edwards, the most sacred piece of airport real estate in the world, the explo-ration of the heavens has vivified not only aeronautics but the world. At special flying events every year at Oshkosh, Watsonville, Blakesburg, Rhinebeck, Old Warden and hundreds of other airports around the world that bond men and women of the air, the magic, the wonder, the spirit of flight comes alive.

As hard as it may be at times to feel the presence of this special element in the crowded concourses of the giant air terminals, it is there. It is to be found in the heart of that dreamer at the boundary fence who is now at the crux of all major air terminal activity, flying and maintaining the transports that whisk us, dare I say, perfunctorily to our destinations. As long as airplanes are taking off and landing, the love of flight must be present.

The Airport

BELOW: Chicago O'Hare International Airport's monumental flow of air traffic sets it apart from other airports. Yet the world's busiest airport is like every other airport in the most fundamental sense. It is a patch of open space, perennially maintained as an unobstructed tract of land for the comings and goings of airplanes. Known as Orchard Place well before the advent of the jet age,

OPPOSITE: As expected for an airport where air traffic is a steady stream, the surrounding airspace is continuously monitored and managed by teams of the world's most professional air traffic controllers. This Chicago Terminal Area Chart is updated and published every six months by the National Ocean Service, a unit of the National Oceanic and Atmospheric Administration, which is part of the U.S. Department of Commerce. A block of airspace known as Class B airspace wraps around the airport

O'Hare's official identifier remains to this day the traditional 'ORD' and all luggage transported to the airport carries tags marked accordingly. This view of contemporary O'Hare from the plateau in the north-west corner of the airport grounds, affectionately referred to as 'the hill' by ground crews, conjures up images of an earlier time when this bustling center of air transportation was

like an upside-down wedding cake, concentric circles emanating from O'Hare like ripples in a pond, each designating a progressively higher floor at which the stringent rules and regulations of Class B airspace apply. Only aircraft with permission from air traffic control may penetrate this extremely congested airspace, and once inside the inner sanctum all are subject to the omnipotent dictates of the controllers.

The radio frequencies covering this airspace are abuzz with a studied mono-

a rural airstrip ensconced amid farmland, prairies and, yes, orchard fields. However much concrete, kerosene, rubber, aluminum and flesh may converge here, it, like any air terminus, will always from some vantage point retain the look and the feel of a stately refuge, albeit for birds with man-made wings.

tone of assigned altitudes and heading commands. There is hardly a gap in the purposeful chatter long enough to hiccup. The relentlessness of these communications and their critical import require, like the script of a good movie, that there be no wasted words. Occasionally, however, the wry barnstormer's wit in some of the airline captains does shine through. O'Hare Tower: 'United three-one-niner, clear for immediate take-off.' United Captain: 'Three-one-niner is steppin' on it.' (*Not for navigation*)

ABOVE: Known by more than sixty-nine million travelers annually as simply 'O'Hare', this airport requires a massive infrastructure of roads and highways to accommodate the incredible volumes of motor traffic.

RIGHT: Unusually artistic billboards greet travelers as they approach O'Hare's terminal buildings. Colorful banners showcasing Chicago's cultural attractions decorate the roadway loop, enhancing O'Hare's ambiance.

RIGHT: To its credit, the airport administration does not perceive O'Hare as an appendage, but rather an integral part of the larger community. A main drive at the airport has been appropriately named after famed aviatrix Bessie Coleman, the first licensed African-American pilot. A daring air show performer and stunt pilot in the 1920s, Coleman lived for a while in Chicago and until her untimely death in a flying accident had regularly visited schools and churches inspiring disadvantaged youngsters with her example of success in aviation. In the background is an ATS (Airport Transit System) vehicle providing passengers with a transportation link between long-term parking lots and terminals via a 2.7-mile elevated guide way.

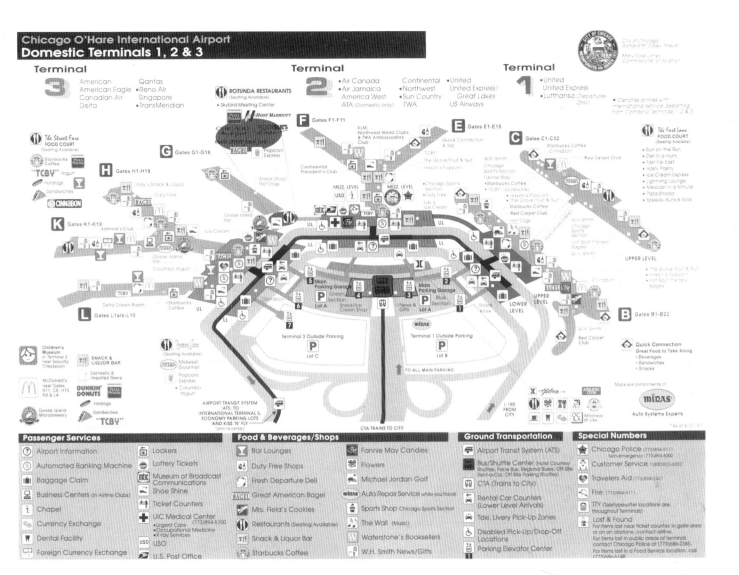

Chicago O'Hare International Airport
Domestic Terminals 1, 2 & 3

Terminal 3
- American
- American Eagle
- Canadian Air
- Delta
- Qantas
- •Reno Air
- Singapore
- •TransMeridian

Terminal 2
- •Air Canada
- •Air Jamaica
- America West
- ATA (Domestic only)
- Continental
- •Northwest
- •Sun Country
- TWA
- •United
- United Express/
  Great Lakes
- US Airways

Terminal 1
- •United
- United Express
- •Lufthansa (Departures Only)

• Denotes airlines with international service departing from Domestic Terminals 1, 2 & 3

Passenger Services

⊙ Airport Information	Lockers
Ⓢ Automated Banking Machine	Lottery Tickets
Baggage Claim	Museum of Broadcast Communications
Business Centers (in Airline Clubs)	Shoe Shine
ⓘ Chapel	Ticket Counters
Currency Exchange	UIC Medical Center (773)894-5100 • Urgent Care • Occupational Medicine • X-ray Services
Dental Facility	USO
Foreign Currency Exchange	U.S. Post Office

Food & Beverages/Shops

Bar Lounges	Fannie May Candies
Duty Free Shops	Flowers
Fresh Departure Deli	Michael Jordan Golf
Great American Bagel	Auto Repair Service while you travel
Mrs. Field's Cookies	Sports Shop Chicago Sports Section
Restaurants (Seating Available)	The Wall (Music)
Snack & Liquor Bar	Waterstone's Booksellers
Starbucks Coffee	W.H. Smith News/Gifts

Ground Transportation

Airport Transit System (ATS)
Bus/Shuttle Center (Hotel Courtesy Shuttles, Pace Bus, Regional Buses, Off-Site Rent-a-Car, Off-Site Parking Shuttles)
CTA (Trains to City)
Rental Car Counters (Lower Level Arrivals)
Taxi, Livery Pick-Up Zones
Disabled Pick-Up/Drop-Off Locations
Parking Elevator Center

Special Numbers

Chicago Police (773)894-9933 Non-emergency (773)894-5000
Customer Service 1(800)832-6352
Travelers Aid (773)894-2427
Fire (773)894-9111
TTY (Teletypewriter locations are throughout Terminal)
Lost & Found For items lost near ticket counter, in gate area or on an airplane, contact airline. For items lost in public areas of terminal, contact Chicago Police at (773)686-2385. For items lost in a Food Service location, call (773)686-6148.

ABOVE: Most of the 190,000 travelers passing through O'Hare on an average day use one of the three voluminous domestic terminals that are interconnected at the center of the airport grounds. O'Hare is a virtual city with a large hotel linked to the domestic terminals by a pedestrian tunnel, more than 10,000 automobile parking spaces, a medical center, a post office, an interdenominational chapel, and virtually every variety of restaurant from ice cream parlors to cocktail lounges. This color-coded map helps travelers navigate through the domestic terminals' maze. (*Map courtesy Chicago Department of Aviation*)

BELOW: Concourses H and K sprout from Terminal 3 to form an efficient 'Y' shape. Turn around time at domestic gates is minimal. The airport has a total of 162 gates and an average of 103 aircraft arrivals or departures each hour.
(*Photo courtesy Chicago Department of Aviation*)

OPPOSITE: O'Hare has seven runways. While adequate on balmy summer days, in the middle of a winter snowstorm arriving flights can get stacked up and traffic on the ground may be logjammed. The longest runway measures two-and-a-half miles and is the preferred departure runway by aircrews operating fully loaded jumbo jets to distant overseas destinations. Airline maintenance facilities and run-up test pads, located in an area known as 'hangar alley', occupy the north-west sector. Cargo operations are concentrated in the south-west sector, known as 'cargo city'. The north-east ramp is the exclusive domain of U.S. military refueling aircraft. The airport's operations are spread over approximately 7,700 acres.
(*Diagram courtesy Jeppesen Sanderson Inc.*)
(*Not for navigation*)

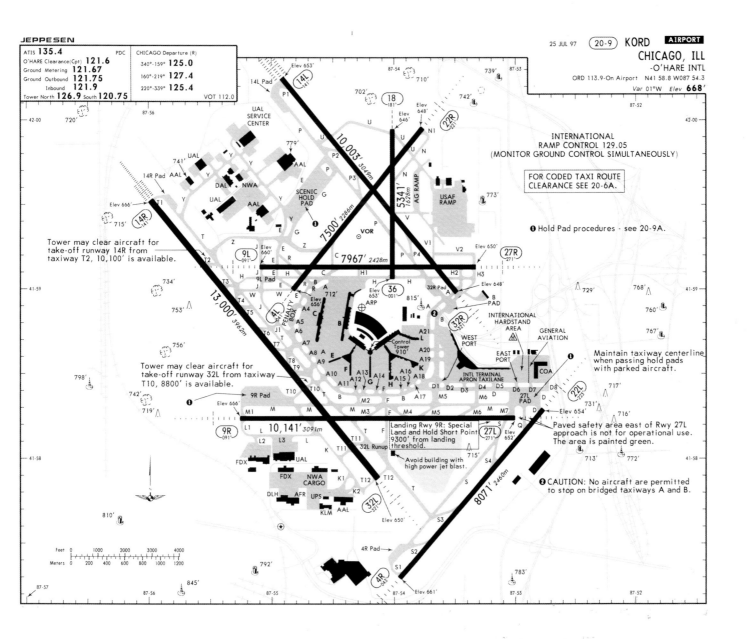

JEPPESEN

25 JUL 97 (20-9) KORD AIRPORT

CHICAGO, ILL
-O'HARE INTL
ORD 113.9-On Airport N41 58.8 W087 54.3
Var 01°W Elev 668'

ATIS 135.4
PDC
O'HARE Clearance(Cpt) 121.6
Ground Metering 121.67
Ground Outbound 121.75
Inbound 121.9
Tower North 126.9 South 120.75

CHICAGO Departure (R)
340°-159° 125.0
160°-219° 127.4
220°-339° 125.4
VOT 112.0

INTERNATIONAL
RAMP CONTROL 129.05
(MONITOR GROUND CONTROL SIMULTANEOUSLY)

FOR CODED TAXI ROUTE
CLEARANCE SEE 20-6A.

❶ Hold Pad procedures - see 20-9A.

UAL SERVICE CENTER

SCENIC HOLD PAD

USAF RAMP

Tower may clear aircraft for take-off runway 14R from taxiway T2, 10,100' is available.

Tower may clear aircraft for take-off runway 32L from taxiway T10, 8800' is available.

PENALTY BOX

Control Tower 910'

INTERNATIONAL HARDSTAND AREA

GENERAL AVIATION

WEST PORT

EAST PORT

COA

INTL TERMINAL APRON TAXILANE

27L PAD

Maintain taxiway centerline when passing hold pads with parked aircraft.

Landing Rwy 9R: Special Land and Hold Short Point 9300' from landing threshold.

Avoid building with high power jet blast.

Paved safety area east of Rwy 27L approach is not for operational use. The area is painted green.

❷ CAUTION: No aircraft are permitted to stop on bridged taxiways A and B.

Feet 0 1000 2000 3000 4000
Meters 0 200 400 600 800 1000 1200

13

ABOVE: When, after World War Two, Orchard Place began slowly to evolve from a Douglas C-54 transport plane manufacturing site to a full-fledged metropolitan commercial airport, aviation visionaries could just begin to imagine the far-flung operations that would characterize Chicago O'Hare International Airport. Serving more than sixty-nine million passengers each year with over 900,000 aircraft operations, the science fiction of the pre-war years became reality at O'Hare. Indeed, futuristic concepts showing a grand aerodrome adjoining a distinctive urban skyline with glittering terminals and sculpturesque towers arcing skyward, sleek transports and gargantuan ships from small towns and exotic locations adorned in the handsome colors of domestic airlines, and international flag carriers criss-crossing overhead in orderly fashion as they decelerate from their typical cruising speeds delineated in fractions of Mach 1 – all are now accepted as commonplace. Seen here are airliners simultaneously arriving and departing under the watchful eye of O'Hare's air traffic controllers in the new control tower (to the right), which replaced the old control tower (to the left).

RIGHT: Shortly after O'Hare replaced Midway as Chicago's primary commercial airport, a formal dedication of the airport in memory of the courageous young Chicagoan was held. President John F. Kennedy, accompanied by long-time Chicago Mayor Richard Daley, laid a wreath at an airport monument commemorating Butch O'Hare as part of the dedication ceremony on 23 March, 1963.
(*Photo courtesy Chicago Department of Aviation*)

ABOVE: It is a commentary of sorts that almost none of the millions of air travelers dashing through O'Hare's terminals have any idea as to the origin of the airport's name. While, of course, the airport's main objective is to provide the flying public with air transport as unfettered as possible, it is to be hoped that somehow along the way passengers could glean at least the bare essentials of the heroic contributions of Lieutenant-Commander Edward H. 'Butch' O'Hare. A naval aviator whose family had settled in Chicago, Butch O'Hare, in the months following the attack on Pearl Harbor, intercepted a formation of Japanese bombers that was en route to the U.S. aircraft carrier *Lexington*. He shot down five of the enemy aircraft and disabled a sixth, thereby saving the ship and its 5,000 sailors from near certain loss. He became the Navy's first ace of World War Two and was awarded the Medal of Honor. Sadly, he was killed the next year on a night fighter mission. Aviation enthusiasts have restored a Grumman F4F-3 Wildcat in the markings of the aircraft piloted by Butch O'Hare in Navy fighter squadron VF-3. As this book went to press, the restored aircraft was permanently mounted on a display pedestal near a heavily trafficked pedestrian walkway.
(*Photo courtesy Chicago Department of Aviation*)

ABOVE AND BELOW: The colors of a rainbow radiate over the world's busiest airport as a morning shower passes to the east giving way to brightening skies.

LEFT: With considerable forward planning Chicago, realizing the eventual need for an expanded commercial airline terminus, began purchasing substantial acreage after World War Two from the War Assets Administration in order to have facilities to handle the burgeoning air traffic. Chicago acquired most of the more than 7,000 acres on its western periphery for only $400 per acre, an amount so unbelievably meager by today's real-estate values that it almost rivals the purchase of Manhattan from the native Americans. All air-side city vehicles at O'Hare are emblazoned with Chicago's official emblem.

BELOW: With the aircraft of more than sixty-five airlines traversing the taxiways at O'Hare, low-mounted warning signs serve as helpful reminders to watch for traffic that may be taxiing nearby.

ABOVE: Despite the enormous volume of traffic, the combined professionalism of flight crews and air traffic controllers usually keeps the stream moving smoothly. It takes acts of nature like heavy snowfall, ice or fog to foster a bottleneck. As the 'commercial aviation capital of the world', there is a mystique pervading O'Hare. Everyone involved in flight operations – including those in the aircraft, those in the control tower and those servicing the aircraft – knows this is a special place with special demands, and their conduct reflects it. There is an unofficial but noticeable effort to try a little harder to make things click. After all, this is O'Hare.

LEFT: More warning signs impart valuable advice just before turning from a taxiway onto a runway.

BELOW: Flames shoot up ferociously and black smoke clouds form as a team of Chicago firefighters practises dousing a simulated airliner fire. Note the dummy aircraft's rounded fuselage and vertical stabilizer. The drama associated with this training is all part of a normal day at O'Hare.

OPPOSITE ABOVE: At the northern tip of the airfield, far removed from the conference rooms and airline clubs in O'Hare's terminals and well out of sight of the 190,000 daily passengers, the Chicago Fire Department regularly performs drills on dummy aircraft hulks to ensure preparedness in the event of an emergency. Here, firefighters from a station in a nearby part of the city get training in passenger extraction techniques should they ever be called in to augment the full-time airport firefighting crews. The training involves locating and removing mannequins from a smoke-clogged fuselage mock-up, which this squad is about to enter. The environment was so realistically hostile in this exercise that one of the firefighters was temporarily overcome by smoke.

ABOVE: Man and nature mix as an airliner glides over the approach lights that are in proximity to a patch of naturally occurring wildflowers.

RIGHT: The old expression 'over the fence' is just as relevant at O'Hare as at any quaint country airfield.

BELOW: Terminal 5 was built expressly for international operations. It has 156 ticket counter positions, six security checkpoints, twenty-one gates and sixty-eight immigration booths capable of processing 4,000 passengers per hour. It is a free-standing building that serves more than six million passengers annually.
(*Photo courtesy Chicago Department of Aviation*)

ABOVE: A sampling of the scope of international flight operations at O'Hare is in view. Like the flags atop the masts of the tall ships in the age of sail, these ships of the sky bear their corporate logos and national insignia on their fins.
(*Photo courtesy Chicago Department of Aviation*)

LEFT: Most international flights at O'Hare have been consolidated in its newest terminal which is devoted solely to foreign air travel. Forty-one airlines operate from what is known as Terminal 5.

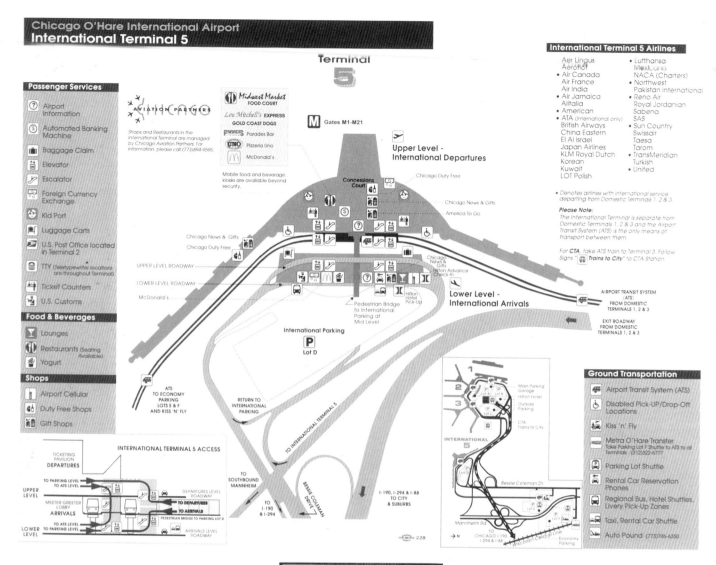

Terminal 5

Passenger Services

- Airport Information
- Automated Banking Machine
- Baggage Claim
- Elevator
- Escalator
- Foreign Currency Exchange
- Kid Port
- Luggage Carts
- U.S. Post Office located in Terminal 2
- TTY (Teletypewriter locations are throughout Terminal)
- Ticket Counters
- U.S. Customs

Food & Beverages

- Lounges
- Restaurants (Seating Available)
- Yogurt

Shops

- Airport Cellular
- Duty Free Shops
- Gift Shops

Aviation Partners

Shops and Restaurants in the International Terminal are managed by Chicago Aviation Partners. For information, please call (773)894-9595.

Midwest Market FOOD COURT

- Lou Mitchell's EXPRESS
- GOLD COAST DOGS
- Parades Bar
- Pizzeria Uno
- McDonald's

Mobile food and beverage kiosks are available beyond security.

M Gates M1–M21

Upper Level - International Departures

Concessions Court

Chicago Duty Free

Chicago News & Gifts

America To Go

Chicago News & Gifts

Chicago Duty Free

UPPER LEVEL ROADWAY

LOWER LEVEL ROADWAY

McDonald's

Pedestrian Bridge to International Parking at Mid Level

Chicago News & Gifts

Hilton Advance Check-In

Hilton Hotel Pick-Up

Lower Level - International Arrivals

International Parking — **P** Lot D

ATS TO ECONOMY PARKING LOTS E & F AND KISS 'N' FLY

RETURN TO INTERNATIONAL PARKING

TO INTERNATIONAL TERMINAL 5

AIRPORT TRANSIT SYSTEM (ATS) FROM DOMESTIC TERMINALS 1, 2 & 3

EXIT ROADWAY FROM DOMESTIC TERMINALS 1, 2 & 3

International Terminal 5 Airlines

- Aer Lingus
- Aeroflot
- Air Canada
- Air France
- Air India
- Air Jamaica
- Alitalia
- American
- ATA (International only)
- British Airways
- China Eastern
- El Al Israel
- Japan Airlines
- KLM Royal Dutch
- Korean
- Kuwait
- LOT Polish
- Lufthansa
- Mexicana
- NACA (Charters)
- Northwest
- Pakistan International
- Reno Air
- Royal Jordanian
- Sabena
- SAS
- Sun Country
- Swissair
- Taesa
- Tarom
- TransMeridian
- Turkish
- United

• Denotes airlines with international service departing from Domestic Terminals 1, 2 & 3.

Please Note:
The International Terminal is separate from Domestic Terminals 1, 2 & 3 and the Airport Transit System (ATS) is the only means of transport between them.

For **CTA**, take ATS train to Terminal 3. Follow Signs "Trains to City" to CTA Station.

INTERNATIONAL TERMINAL 5 ACCESS

TICKETING PAVILION DEPARTURES

UPPER LEVEL
- TO PARKING LEVEL TO ATS LEVEL
- PARKING LEVEL
- DEPARTURES LEVEL ROADWAY

MEETER GREETER LOBBY ARRIVALS
- TO DEPARTURES
- TO ARRIVALS

LOWER LEVEL
- TO ATS LEVEL TO PARKING LEVEL
- PEDESTRIAN BRIDGE TO PARKING LOT D
- ARRIVALS LEVEL ROADWAY

TO SOUTHBOUND MANNHEIM

TO I-190 & I-294

BESSIE COLEMAN DRIVE

I-190, I-294 & I-88 TO CITY & SUBURBS

228

Ground Transportation

- Airport Transit System (ATS)
- Disabled Pick-UP/Drop-Off Locations
- Kiss 'n' Fly
- Metra O'Hare Transfer — Take Parking Lot F Shuttle to ATS to all Terminals (312)322-6777
- Parking Lot Shuttle
- Rental Car Reservation Phones
- Regional Bus, Hotel Shuttles, Livery Pick-Up Zones
- Taxi, Rental Car Shuttle
- Auto Pound (773)746-6350

Main Parking Garage
Hilton Hotel
Outside Parking
CTA Trains to City

INTERNATIONAL 5

Bessie Coleman Dr.

Mannheim Rd.

TO CHICAGO I-190, I-294 & I-88

Wisconsin Central Line

Economy Parking

→ N

RIGHT: When opened in 1993, the International Terminal was christened with words of warmth and welcome, reminding visitors that Chicago, as the largest city between the coasts of the U.S., is a 'crossroads' and a 'gateway'.

Building on Chicago's legacy as the crossroads of the nation and America's gateway to the world

Chicago O'Hare International Terminal
Dedicated May 27, 1993

Richard M. Daley
Mayor of Chicago

OPPOSITE ABOVE: Covering 1.2 million square feet (111,500m²), the International Terminal is a massive structure accommodating an average of seventy-five departures each day. The monorail-style Airport Transit System can move passengers to the domestic terminals in two to four minutes. From there, subway trains (known also as elevated trains, or simply the 'el') connect with Chicago's downtown in approximately forty minutes.
(*Map courtesy Chicago Department of Aviation*)

ABOVE: International carriers line up at Terminal 5. More than sixty-six international destinations are served in non-stop or one-stop flights from O'Hare.

ABOVE: As expected at the world's busiest airport, the general aviation ramp is occupied by some pretty high-end equipment. This tri-motor Dassault Falcon is taxiing to a departure runway.

OPPOSITE BELOW: This Canadair Challenger is headed for the general aviation fixed-base operator, almost certainly to deplane corporate executives who have come to town for a quick business meeting. By afternoon, the jet had departed.

OPPOSITE ABOVE: An old Lockheed L-1011 in a two-tone scheme, perhaps awaiting completion of a paint job, taxis towards 'cargo city'. One of the thrills of O'Hare is that in time you are bound to see some unusual combinations of hardware and markings.

BELOW: O'Hare has become so busy that many observers believe it has reached the saturation point and that the only answer to the expanding air traffic is to establish another major hub airport somewhere in the outer reaches of the metroplex. (*Photo courtesy Chicago Department of Aviation*)

OPPOSITE ABOVE: The constant flow of traffic keeps the ramp at O'Hare humming. Because more than 100 flights take place every hour, a veritable sea of concrete is needed to accommodate the incoming and outgoing airliners (*Photo courtesy Chicago Department of Aviation*)

OPPOSITE BELOW: O'Hare has the disadvantage of being located in America's snow-belt. Winters in the heartland of America are ordinarily harsh. While recent winters have been unusually mild, perhaps owing to the effects of the El Nino phenomenon, in the past some storms have practically immobilized the city and surrounding suburbs. No matter how severe the snowfall, O'Hare's Airfield Operations unit keeps the runways and taxiways open with massive plows and sweepers. These dedicated crews take great pride in removing layer after layer of snow to ensure that the traffic never stops moving at the world's busiest airport.

ABOVE: A highway running through the airport might present a problem if this were anywhere else but O'Hare. The solution was simple: just build taxiways over the highway.

LEFT: At its core, O'Hare is an airfield, albeit a very big one. Its maze of runways and taxiways is outlined in a continuum of markers, color-coded lights, and high-tech navigation/communications devices.

BELOW: Flights at O'Hare receive a curious blend of individual attention and processing by rote. Each arriving and departing flight must fit into an established air traffic channel, but at the same time no two flights are exactly alike. Key to O'Hare's success is the airport's regular operating system combined with an ability to adapt. Handling mind-boggling numbers of airplanes and passengers has become routine for O'Hare.

BELOW: The tell-tale clover leaf identifies this huge airliner as belonging to Ireland's Aer Lingus. One of the first operators of the Airbus A330, Aer Lingus acquired three in 1994.

OPPOSITE ABOVE: Quebec-based Air Canada operates a dwindling number of Douglas DC-9 airliners. This one, in the company's old colors, features the ubiquitous maple leaf on the fin.

OPPOSITE BELOW: Reflecting the modernization of its fleet is this short- to medium-range Airbus sporting the airline's new paint scheme.

OPPOSITE ABOVE: Air Canada has begun operating the Canadair RJ-100 airliner, and has a number of additional units on order. With a seating capacity of fifty, these twin jets are geared for the increasingly sophisticated regional market.

OPPOSITE BELOW: Planning to phase out its DC-9s by 1998, this example nevertheless is decorated in the current colors of Air Canada.

BELOW: An airline workhorse for many years, the Boeing 727 labors on for Air Jamaica. The aircraft is fittingly emblazoned with a Caribbean motif, which becomes all the more inviting to Chicagoans the closer winter approaches.

ABOVE: Italian flag carrier Alitalia operates Boeing 767-300 aircraft on routes to O'Hare. This example has started its take-off roll on runway 32R.

BELOW: This sleek Boeing 757 is in conventional America West Airlines livery. The airline has had its financial ups and downs, but seems to have carved out a niche for itself in servicing its home town of Phoenix.

ABOVE: Among the most eye-catching of paint schemes, this America West Airlines Boeing 757, dubbed *City of Phoenix*, is adorned in the colors popularized by the local basketball team. The aircraft is taxying to a jetway as air traffic technicians peer out from O'Hare's distinctive control tower.

ABOVE: O'Hare has considerable commuter airline traffic, including flights by ATR-42s operated by American Eagle. Turn-around time at the terminal is quick.

RIGHT: This American Eagle ATR-42 is equally at home at a busy hub like O'Hare or at quiet, small-town airports that are the bread and butter of regional airline operations.

ABOVE: The standard commuter airliner configuration of a twin turboprop provides for greater fuel efficiency and generally better short-field performance over jet competitors. On shorter routes, these aircraft have proved to be economical. With advances in small turbines and with consumers' expectations rising, pure jets in downsized versions are catching up with turboprops on regional routes.

ABOVE: American Eagle also operates the Saab 340, a twin turboprop that emerged from the Swedish manufacturer in the mid-1980s. American Eagle is the regional airline unit of air transport giant American Airlines.

BELOW: An elongated variant, the ATR-72, known in the American Eagle fleet as the Super ATR, has a much greater load capacity than the older ATR-42.

ABOVE: Though based in Dallas, Texas, American Airlines has made O'Hare one of its major hubs. The company operates a whopping seventy-five Fokker F-100s.

LEFT: This American Airlines F-100, called a 'Luxury Jet' by the company, undergoes routine servicing between flights.

ABOVE: Each airliner requires enormous amounts of support from baggage handlers, caterers, fuelers, linemen, mechanics, janitorial technicians, etc. These service personnel swarm over the aircraft to prepare them for turn-around as fast as possible. Airliners are revenue-producing only when airworthy and airborne.

ABOVE: With up to ninety-seven passengers onboard, the flight deck crew of two will soon level off and cruise the Fokker F-100 at an altitude of up to 35,000 feet and a speed of up to 367 mph.

BELOW: Indisputably a marvelous airplane from both economic and aesthetic viewpoints, the Fokker F-100, like the entire product line, has come to a permanent production halt because of the manufacturer's ailing financial condition.

OPPOSITE: The McDonnell Douglas MD-80 aircraft represents the single most numerous type in the American Airlines fleet. The company operates 260 of the DC-9 derivative.

ABOVE: This view shows the dominance of American Airlines at Terminal 3. The investment in aircraft is tremendous with everything from Fokker F-100s to McDonnell Douglas MD-80s to Boeing 757s represented. Note that aircraft tend to be clustered by type. (*Photo courtesy Chicago Department of Aviation*)

ABOVE: Even at busy O'Hare, aircraft get their moment of solitude when in the concluding stages of final approach. There are no commands being emitted from the tower and, through expert air traffic coordination, there are no other aircraft to be seen at this particular instant in time. This is when the flight crew transitions from 'managing' a high-tech cockpit to flying their airplane like aviators of old.

BELOW: The MD-80 greases onto the pavement. As the rubber contacts the hard surface, a puff of smoke becomes visible aft of the main landing gear. Late at night, when O'Hare's traffic tapers off, cleaning crews apply a solvent to remove the residue of rubber from runway surfaces.

ABOVE: The MD-80 was developed as a follow-on to the successful DC-9. With the great market acceptance of the DC-9, it was only logical that the manufacturer would seek to capitalize on the basic aircraft configuration. The concept called for stretching the fuselage, increasing the capacity and uprating the engines. The aircraft was called the '80' in recognition of its expected in-service entry date – 1980. The letter identifiers were changed from 'DC' to 'MD' reflecting Douglas's merger into what became known as McDonnell Douglas. Recently, in yet another round of consolidation within the aerospace industry, Boeing has acquired the company.

ABOVE: American Airlines expected to reduce the number of 727s it operates from seventy to only thirty-five by 1998. The three-person flight deck has become anachronistic and is not economically competitive with more modern airliners.

RIGHT: Boeing followed its transcontinental 707 airliner with the smaller, shorter-range 727. The 727 design is well over thirty years old, the last models having been built in 1984. While a very successful airliner, its use is rapidly receding.

OPPOSITE: In the evening, Chicago's glimmering lights provide a fitting backdrop for part of the American Airlines operation at O'Hare.
(*Photo courtesy Chicago Department of Aviation*)

ABOVE: Signifying a new era in commercial airliners, the Boeing 757 makes use of a twin-jet configuration. The 757 has sophisticated cockpit instrumentation allowing for a two-person flight crew.

BELOW: Powerplant options on the 757 include Rolls-Royce and Pratt & Whitney turbofans with maximum thrust ranging from 37,400 lb to 41,700 lb.

OPPOSITE: This view of the underside planform highlights the narrow body of the 757 as well as the swept wings and horizontal stabilizers.

ABOVE: The narrow-body 757 has a sleek appearance, making it among the most attractive of current-generation airliners. On the other hand, travelers do not always appreciate the tight quarters – six abreast seating with a center aisle.

RIGHT: American Airlines is noted for efficiently running one of the world's largest and most diverse fleets of aircraft. Watching expenditures carefully, the company realized that there were savings to be made by leaving large sections of its airliners' fuselages unpainted. Not only is there a saving in painting materials and labor, but the aircraft weigh a little less and enjoy a slight performance improvement.

ABOVE: A development of the late 1970s/early 1980s, the Boeing 767 is a wide-body airliner. An extended-range version was produced for longer routes. This American Airlines 767 is being serviced at the International Terminal, where all arriving international flights, even of domestic airlines, must park for Customs clearance.

OPPOSITE ABOVE: Departing runway 32R, conveniently located for the airliners using the International Terminal, this American Airlines 767 is seen rising above the silhouette of Chicago's tallest building, the Sears Tower, in the distance.

OPPOSITE BELOW: As with other modern aircraft in its fleet, American Airlines continues to add 767s. The number is scheduled to increase from seventy-one in 1997 to seventy-four in 1998. Interestingly, the larger seating capacity of such wide bodies as the 767 allows American Airlines to carry more passengers with fewer aircraft.

ABOVE: With three engines the McDonnell Douglas MD-11 is a rarity among long-range airliners currently in production. American Airlines has been actually reducing its use of the type, and by 1998 is scheduled to be operating only ten.

ABOVE: Seen at O'Hare's 'cargo city', this older model Boeing 747 is operated as a freighter under licence by Atlas Air of Golden, Colorado. Note the artwork on the fin depicting the mythological figure Atlas carrying the world on his shoulders.

RIGHT: Part of the air freight enterprise managed by entrepreneur and former race car driver Conrad 'Connie' Kalitta, Willow Run-based American International Airways operates fourteen cargo variants of the Boeing 727 like this one with virtually no side windows.

ABOVE AND LEFT: As one of the world's largest airlines, the operations of British Airways would not be complete without service to O'Hare. Here, one of its Boeing 747-200s roars to life on takeoff from runway 14R, O'Hare's longest runway at 13,000 feet.

OPPOSITE ABOVE: Calgary, Alberta-based Canadian Airlines flies the Boeing 737-200.

OPPOSITE BELOW: Continental Airlines of Houston, Texas is among the major U.S. airlines. It has encountered its share of financial bumps, but is on a steady course for now. This DC-9-30 is one of a dwindling number in Continental's fleet, which is being modernized with newer aircraft.

ABOVE: The Boeing 737 is regarded by many as one of today's outstanding airline workhorses. The type is the most common in Continental's service inventory.

ABOVE AND BELOW: Delta Air Lines has a significant presence at O'Hare. Long regarded as a leader in passenger service and comfort, Delta operates a large fleet of MD-80s. It has also been adding the new MD-90, a re-engined version of the MD-80.

ABOVE: From its headquarters in Atlanta, Georgia, Delta manages an airliner fleet numbering well in excess of 500 aircraft, including the wide-body Boeing 767.

BELOW: Like many big U.S. domestic air carriers, Delta has long operated the venerable Boeing 727. Rather than simply junk its fleet of over a hundred 727s, Delta has embarked on an effort to outfit many of them with hushkits to improve their environmental acceptability in the years to come.

ABOVE: Its design dating from the 1950s, the Douglas DC-8 was a leading cross-country and intercontinental airliner more than a generation ago. Today, almost all remaining examples in use have been converted to cargo haulers. It is a treat to see them still in operation. This DC-8, parked at O'Hare's 'cargo city', belongs to Emery Worldwide, a heavy freight carrier with a major hub at the airport in Dayton, Ohio.

ABOVE: Package delivery service Federal Express operates one of the largest non-passenger jet fleets. Adorned in its well-recognized colors, this FedEx freighter is an Airbus A300-600F. The cargo-handling facilities at O'Hare were built to accommodate air freighters in an area on the airport's grounds sufficiently removed from the passenger terminals so as not to interfere with the operation of passenger airliners.

ABOVE AND OPPOSITE BELOW: After a long trans-Pacific journey, the ramp of Terminal 5 must look very refreshing to the passengers on board this Japan Airlines 747–400. As soon as the aircraft finishes taxying, the jetway will be extended to allow the passengers to deplane.

LEFT AND OPPOSITE BELOW: Airlines have identified themselves with distinctive markings on their aircraft for as long as can be remembered. Here, the logo for Japan Airlines is emblazoned on the fin of a Boeing 747-400. Cleverly, the company's acronym is repeated on the aircraft's winglets.

RIGHT: An airline that traces its beginnings to 1919, KLM Royal Dutch Airlines operates various models of the Boeing 747.

BELOW AND OPPOSITE: One of the first customers for the Boeing 747, KLM has continued to buy the aircraft in its later derivatives. The epitome of the jumbo jet, the 747 soldiers on as a major contributor to airline success on long, heavily traveled routes. This 747 gains speed on its take-off roll, causing moisture from a morning sprinkle to form a spray-like mist in its wake. KLM has named this aircraft in honor of Charles E. Kingsford Smith.

RIGHT: Strategically positioned in the rapidly expanding Asian market, Korean Air Lines operates a large fleet of wide-body aircraft.

BELOW: Earlier model 747s are used by the cargo operation of Korean Air Lines. This jumbo jet is taxying to O'Hare's self-contained cargo area.

ABOVE: On passenger routes, Korean Air Lines operates this Boeing 747-400. The aircraft is seen landing on O'Hare's runway 32L.

RIGHT: The Lufthansa tail logo is a common sight at major airport hubs around the world since the airline is one of the leading international air carriers.

BELOW AND OPPOSITE ABOVE: Cargo operations are a significant portion of Lufthansa's business. This Boeing 747 cargo hauler arrives at O'Hare's runway 32L. Note extended flaps, main landing gear rubber burn, and nose-high attitude. Everything is in sync for a smooth landing.

OPPOSITE BELOW: Having attained take-off speed and rising into the sky, this Lufthansa 747-400 at nearly 870,000 lb remains buoyant and graceful.

ABOVE AND BELOW: A relative newcomer to the Lufthansa fleet is the Airbus A340, a four-engine airliner with an extended-range capability. Lufthansa was one of the type's introduction customers in 1993.

ABOVE AND BELOW: Chicago has a thriving Polish community, many of whose members enjoy visiting relatives and sight-seeing in their ancestral homeland. LOT provides a direct link for these and other travelers.

ABOVE AND BELOW: The Mexican air carrier Mexicana Airlines has weathered financial difficulties in recent years, and flies newly obtained Boeing 757s. The artwork on the fin is a real head-turner.

ABOVE AND BELOW: Northwest Airlines, one of the major airlines in the U.S., bounced back from near bankruptcy to become extraordinarily profitable. Such dramatic swings in airline company fortunes have become common since the days of deregulation. The DC-9 is old and predictable. Northwest still operates many of the type, and plans to retrofit a large percentage of them with hushkits.

OPPOSITE ABOVE: Another elder and reliable workhorse in the Northwest stable is the Boeing 727. This example makes a morning departure from O'Hare.

ABOVE AND OPPOSITE BELOW: The Boeing 757 is an integral part of the Northwest Airlines fleet. Climbing above O'Hare's sprawling grounds, the flight crew quickly retracts the landing gear to improve the aircraft's aerodynamics and enhance its climb performance.

ABOVE, BELOW AND OPPOSITE ABOVE: In this sequence, a Sabena A340 builds up take-off speed on runway 32R. As the aircraft gains momentum, the flight crew pulls back on the controls and the nose lifts off the pavement. With all systems go, the aircraft is established on a standard climb-out for this routine early-evening departure. Sabena is the state-controlled airline of Belgium.

BELOW: This SAS 767 has just pulled away from its gate at O'Hare's International Terminal and is taxying to a departure runway. Note the bright stripes on the forward fuselage which represent the colors of the three Scandinavian countries that own portions of SAS (derived from Scandinavian Airlines System). The flags of Denmark, Norway and Sweden are emblazoned on the aft fuselage.

RIGHT: Zürich-based Swissair is an international air carrier with an established presence at O'Hare. The airline operates the MD-11 on routes to Chicago.

BELOW: Swissair's five Boeing 747s include this one on the tarmac at O'Hare.

ABOVE: Singapore Airlines is well positioned to take advantage of the growth in commercial air traffic in the Pacific rim. The company has long favored the Boeing 747. Here, a 747-400 eases down for a landing at O'Hare.

ABOVE AND BELOW: TransMeridian is a smaller air carrier whose fleet includes this Boeing 727. The aircraft is parked on a pad near the general aviation ramp at O'Hare.

Note the internal stepladder unfolded from the aircraft's tailcone. Such exit systems were regularly used until security concerns forced their discontinuance on most flights.

TransMeridian operates newer aircraft like this Airbus A320. Note that the airline's logo on the fin is repeated on the outboard engine nacelle.

ABOVE AND BELOW: A contrast of the old and new: DC-9 derivatives are seen here in both the traditional and the recently adopted paint schemes of Trans World Airlines. The earlier motif involved simply white with red trim, whereas the current decoration is a sophisticated multi-tone trim arrangement with a splash of gold stenciling.

ABOVE AND BELOW: As an older member of the commercial airline fraternity and a company that fell victim to the leveraged buy-out wars in the aftermath of deregulation, TWA has been saddled with a fairly aged fleet. These Boeing 727s point to the sky on take-off from O'Hare.

ABOVE AND BELOW: If stabilizing the company upon emergence from bankruptcy were not enough, TWA has really had its hands full trying to recover from the mysterious break-up of one of its international flights off the eastern U.S. coast in the mid-1990s. TWA has moved to modernize its fleet and promote an image of commitment to passenger service.

This 727 collects its landing gear and banks towards its course heading, hopefully above the weather where the sailing is smooth.

ABOVE: In 1994, Turkish Airlines received its first Airbus A340. To accommodate international airliners using runway 14L/32R, two taxiway bridges (known as Alpha and Bravo) allow aircraft to transit over a main airport access highway (I-190). All but the most seasoned motorists stomp on their brakes and peer above to catch a glimpse of the airliners moving across these unusual overpasses.

ABOVE: A Beech 1900D twin turboprop operated by United Express is shown on climb-out from O'Hare. This regional airliner is an enlarged version of the earlier model. The hunchback fuselage shape was adopted to give passengers in the cabin more headroom. Note the registration number ending in 'UX' for United Express.

LEFT AND NEXT PAGE: A rare sight is the British Aerospace ATP (Advanced Turboprop), a big twin-engine regional airliner introduced in 1988 amid much fanfare. The aircraft has a slow cruising speed which puts it at a competitive disadvantage to other regional airliners. The ATP never quite caught on with commuter airlines, and these examples operated under the United Express banner at O'Hare are among the small number that can be found in use in the U.S.

ABOVE: A more widely used type from the British Aerospace drafting tables is the family of regional airliners spawned by the BAe 146. The series has evolved into the product line known as the Avro Regional Jets.

The basic configuration has made use of an unconventional regional airliner design: a high wing, T-tail and four jet engines slung under the wing.

OPPOSITE ABOVE: By the key measure of revenue passenger miles flown in a given year, United Airlines is the largest airline in the world. The company employs more than 81,000 people and operates a fleet of over 560 aircraft. As would be expected of an airline headquartered in suburban Chicago, United has a major presence at O'Hare.

OPPOSITE BELOW: When United transitioned to its current paint scheme of blue and gray, it met with mixed reviews. With the passage of time, it has become increasingly accepted.

ABOVE: As this Boeing 727 prepares for touchdown, O'Hare's International Terminal is bracketed in the background.

OPPOSITE ABOVE: Not yet converted to the current paint scheme, this United 727 sports the old white base color with the familiar orange, red and blue trim.

OPPOSITE BELOW: As this United 727 takes off, the voluminous maintenance facilities and administrative field offices of several airlines are visible in the background. Referred to by O'Hare veterans as 'hangar alley', this corner of the airport is a beehive of activity as technicians scramble through the night to prepare airliners for service.

ABOVE: The Boeing 727 has been compared to the legendary Douglas DC-3, a sturdy and trustworthy airplane that served well beyond its expected service life carrying passengers to varied destinations in the livery of innumerable airlines around the world. With the current United Airlines colors adorning this aircraft, it looks almost as good as new. In any event, this 727 is good for a lot more cycles before consignment to a desert boneyard.

OPPOSITE ABOVE: The Boeing 737-200 first entered the United inventory in the late 1960s. The type, still in operation, is being phased out of service, while newer models in the same family remain in service.

OPPOSITE BELOW: Although wearing the old colors of United Airlines, this is a newer or upgraded model of the 737, as is evident from the engines. Unlike the tubular Pratt & Whitney JT8Ds, this aircraft is powered by the pod-like CFM International CFM56-3s.

ABOVE: This view of a Boeing 737-200 exposes the older JT8D turbofans. Aftermarket installers offer hushkits to make these aircraft more acceptable to noise-sensitive communities. Some airlines consider it cost-effective to make this investment since it is a fraction of the cost of a new 737.

OPPOSITE ABOVE: The differences between the old and the new powerplants become obvious when comparing these CFM56-3 engines to the JT8D engines on the 737-200.

OPPOSITE BELOW: A United 737-200 throttles back as it approaches the moment of touchdown. Boeing built a total of 1,144 units of the 737-200 during a period of about twenty years.

ABOVE: The Boeing 737 has labored on since the first production model entered revenue service in 1968. With new variants in the works, there is no end in sight for this stalwart of the airlines.

OPPOSITE ABOVE: Sporting the current United Airlines paint scheme, this 737 makes an early-morning departure from O'Hare's runway 32L.

OPPOSITE BELOW: The impact of O'Hare on the national transportation system and the economy is overwhelming. It is estimated that O'Hare, along with its sister airport Midway on the southern tip of the metroplex, generates 339,000 jobs in the region and accounts for no less than $14.7 billion in economic activity. If inclement weather causes flight operations at O'Hare to sneeze, the flight operations across the rest of the country catch a cold.

ABOVE: O'Hare in some ways is an oasis amid urban/suburban sprawl. Development of one kind or another has mushroomed in virtually every direction, but the plot of ground dedicated to the airport remains flat, open and clear. In the middle of it, one of man's most ingenious inventions operates thousands of times every day without so much as a second thought. The miracle of flight and the beauty of man's noble interaction with nature can best be appreciated from remote corners of the airfield, like this grassy knoll east of runway 22L.

ABOVE: The success of the 737 has prompted Boeing to offer a corporate version of the aircraft to compete with top-of-the-line, purpose-built corporate jets like the Gulfstream. The latest airline version is the 737–800. Seen here is a 737 in the 300/500 series.

BELOW AND OPPOSITE ABOVE: United Airlines has begun to add growing numbers of Airbus A320 and A319 airliners to its fleet. These aircraft are readily distinguishable from the competing Boeing 737 because of their winglets.

OPPOSITE BELOW: First entering commercial airline service in 1983, the 757 has been a steady seller for Boeing after a sluggish start.

ABOVE: United 757s take-off and climb from O'Hare. The airline has been a bit of a maverick in that it is majority owned by the employees and led by an executive with an automotive industry background.

BELOW: The Boeing 757 is the second most common aircraft type in the United Airlines fleet. The company operates more than ninety of these airliners.

ABOVE: United DC-10 takes to the sky. The wide-bodies can seat over 300 passengers.

LEFT: Concourses B and C handle most of United's flights. The concourses are connected by an underground pedestrian walkway. Standing by itself, longitudinally-shaped Concourse C is sometimes called 'the banana'.

ABOVE: A United DC-10 in the company's current paint scheme leaves O'Hare on a long-range route.

RIGHT: Named *Working Together*, this United 777 has the fitting registration number 'N777UA' denoting both the aircraft type and the initials of its operator. When aloft, the sheer size of the advanced 777 is enough to impress.

ABOVE: Crossing over one of O'Hare's two taxiway bridges is a Boeing 777, the ultimate in size and sophistication for a twin-engine airliner. The wingspan is nearly 200 feet, which translates into about two-thirds the length of a football field. Note the shadow cast by the huge wing.

RIGHT: In the days before deregulation, the U.S. had just two major international air carriers - Pan Am and TWA. Now international markets are serviced by a number of U.S. airlines, and their corporate logos, like this vibrant United Airlines example, have become synonymous with the country from whence they come.

BELOW: In 1995, United Airlines became the first operator to take delivery of the Boeing 777, a breakthrough airliner whose design and construction entailed revolutionary processes.

ABOVE: Taking its place alongside other aircraft servicing foreign routes, this United 777 has had its passengers disembark at O'Hare's International Terminal.

OPPOSITE ABOVE: With over 560 aircraft in its fleet and with O'Hare serving as one of its major hubs, United conducts a dizzying array of flight operations. Here, one of its many airliners departs O'Hare.

OPPOSITE BELOW: Weighing as much as 870,000 lb, this United 747-400 thunders aloft from one of O'Hare's departure runways.

ABOVE: The grand-daddy of international airliners is the Boeing 747. Some versions can carry more than 500 passengers. This 747 is still in United's old colors.

OPPOSITE ABOVE AND BELOW: One of the big domestic airlines making a comeback from treacherous financial times is U·S Airways. Its fleet of nearly 400 aircraft includes many Boeing 737s. These examples reflect the company's former colors and carry its former name, USAir.

LEFT: The largest of the package delivery service companies, United Parcel Service operates a fleet of nearly 200 freighter jets.

BELOW: This Boeing 767-300F is being serviced at the UPS freight terminal at O'Hare's 'cargo city'. Note the row of pallets in the foreground.

OPPOSITE ABOVE: Inflight refueling aircraft are based at O'Hare's military facility, which is located in a remote area in the airport's north-east corner. This Illinois Air National Guard KC-135 crosses one of the taxiway bridges on its way back to base after landing.

OPPOSITE BELOW: Reflecting the new direction of the airline, a radical change in the prior paint scheme has been adopted. Also, the new name of U·S Airways prominently stands out. Note that instead of corporate initials adorning the fin, the company's patriotic name is represented by a stylized American flag.

ABOVE: At dusk another surge in activity overtakes O'Hare as business travelers hurry to return home after a full day of meetings and vacationers get off work to start their pre-planned holiday trips. The last rays of sun cast a warm glow over O'Hare's busy operations. (*Photo courtesy Chicago Department of Aviation*)

ABOVE: Silhouetted against a magnificent hue, this Boeing 727 is sequenced for landing at the world's busiest airport. Despite the hectic pace of flight operations at O'Hare, it is possible to capture moments of serenity. (*Photo courtesy Chicago Department of Aviation*)

RIGHT: Bustling Chicago O'Hare International Airport still has time to extend a 'thank you' to its daily contingent of 190,000 passengers.